CONSTRUCTION PEOPLE

POEMS SELECTED BY
Lee Bennett Hopkins

ILLUSTRATED BY
Ellen Shi

WORDSONG

AN IMPRINT OF BOYDS MILLS & KANE
NEW YORK

To Marilyn J. Filarecki, who served as assistant project manager at Pavarini McGovern, New York, NY, during construction of the iconic skyscraper at 505 5th Avenue. Thank you for the unforgettable journey through the building prior to its opening.
—LBH

To all those tirelessly working moms and dads
—ES

ACKNOWLEDGMENTS

The publisher thanks Marilyn J. Filarecki, who served as assistant project manager at Pavarini McGovern, for reviewing the text and illustrations for this book.

Thanks are due to the following for use of works in this collection:
Curtis Brown, Ltd., for "What Will I Become?" and "What I Am" by Rebecca Kai Dotlich, copyright © 2020 by Rebecca Kai Dotlich; "Backhoe Operator" by Georgia Heard, copyright © 2020 by Georgia Heard; "Elevator Installers" by Lee Bennett Hopkins, copyright © 2020 by Lee Bennett Hopkins; "Crane Operator" by Amy Ludwig VanDerwater, copyright © 2020 by Amy Ludwig VanDerwater. All used by permission of Curtis Brown, Ltd.

All other works are used by permission of the respective poets, who control all rights. All poems are copyright © 2020: "Architect" by Denver Butson; "Construction Project Manager" by Matt Forrest Esenwine; "Cement Speaks" by Ralph Fletcher; "Plumbers" by Charles Ghigna; "Glaziers" by Joan Bransfield Graham; "Carpenters" by B. J. Lee; "Electricians" by J. Patrick Lewis; "Dump Truck Drivers" by Darren Sardelli; "Song of the Welders" by Allan Wolf.

For information about permission to reproduce selections from this book, contact permissions@bmkbooks.com.

WordSong
An Imprint of Boyds Mills & Kane
wordsongpoetry.com
Printed in China

ISBN: 978-1-68437-361-1
Library of Congress Control Number: 20199939491

First edition
10 9 8 7 6 5 4 3 2 1

The text is set in Neutraface Text.
The titles are set in Claire Hand.
The illustrations are digital.

CONTENTS

WHAT WILL I BECOME?

Rebecca Kai Dotlich

I will rise

mingled with dirt and dust,
rock and air as they plan me,
pound me, pour me.

Constructed with concrete,
blueprints, time sheets—
I will be window-wrapped,
glazed steep with glass.

They will chisel me, drill me,
wire me, weld me.
They will cram me
with copper and clips,
pulleys and pipes.

A skeleton of rods and steel,
built by muscle and brain—
through rain, wind, and snow

I will rise.

Where fog swirls,
   where rain clouds swell,
      where thunder cracks and cries

I will rise,

overlooking sand and sea,
with nothing but sky

      staring back
            at
            me.

(EAST SIDE VIEW)

5

ARCHITECT
Denver Butson

every building
every barn or office tower
every house or high-rise
every tall building
that climbs through clouds
and scrapes the sky
has two jobs

one
to keep things out—
rain
wind
dirt
bugs—
so whatever is inside
stays dry
warm
clean
without bugs!

two
to keep love inside
love
dreams
plans and meetings
play
laughter
and did I mention dreams?

the architect thought
as she does every time
she looks at the earth
her building would rise out of
and the sky
her building would rise into

just like she did
when she was a little girl
designing and building
her first castle
in the sand.

SEDIMENT STUDY

1.
2.
3.

BACKHOE OPERATOR
Georgia Heard

Excavating vacant land,
my bucket digs through clay and sand.

Sinking teeth in solid ground
cupping earth pound by pound.

Gripping silver levers tight,
swivel loader left and right.

I scoop a hole deep and wide,
dumping dirt from side to side.

Week by week I sweat and toil,
layer by layer unearth more soil.

Shifting, shoveling—final run.
Turn off the engine, my job done.

Out of a pit of soil and rock,
a skyscraper will sit on this city block.

DUMP TRUCK DRIVERS
Darren Sardelli

We're the ones who drive the dump trucks
bulky, big, and bright—
providing help for vehicles
and workers on this site.

It's fun to watch them fill our trucks
with massive mounds of dirt.
This makes us think of brownie mix
(we use to make dessert).

By clearing waste, removing rocks,
and filling holes with sand,
we create a safe environment,
we help smooth out the land.

*BEEP BEEP SCREEEEECH
HARUUUUMFFFFF FA LUMFFFFF*

are thrilling sounds to hear.
Pull the lever—

VRRRR VRRRR VRRRR.

The tilting makes us cheer.

We're here to back up builders
as they work on their creation.
Our caring contributions
help them build a strong foundation.

CEMENT SPEAKS
Ralph Fletcher

Nothing about me is speedy.
Mixing? Pouring? Drying?
Slow, slow, slow.
That's how I go.

The enormous mixing drum rumbles
round and round,
     tossing me up and down,
       but now my time has come.

Set up the discharge chute!
Tilt back the mixing drum
     s l o w l y
pour me out
like elephant-gray pancake batter.

Now workers take over
    pulling, pushing me,
      raking and making me
        smooth as glass.

When I'm fully dry I'll be rock-solid
though that will take a week at least.
Now there's nothing to do but wait.

Ropes around me warn:

KEEP OFF!

Though today a robin landed on me
and left behind four tiny footprints,
like an artist signing her masterpiece.

CRANE OPERATOR

Amy Ludwig VanDerwater

In hard hat and boots
you climb toward sky.
Your cab is an office
stationed on high.

You check to be sure
your machine is now ready.
Every pulley fully safe.
Every cable stable, steady.
Not too windy, to be sure.
Counterweights? All secure.

You inspect
each switch
each section
of your crane
for our protection.

Bit-by-bit you build with steel.
I stare. I wonder. Do you feel
alone all day at such a height?
Do heavy things seem light?

You watch for signals.
You are careful, swift.
Shift after shift
    you lift.
       You lift.

SONG OF THE WELDERS

Allan Wolf

We build the bones that hold the shell.
We are the wizards of the weld.

We are the I-beam climbers
the show-up-on-timers
who rise, at first bell, into structures
by ladder, scaffold, and harness.

We are splicers, joiners,
slicers, cutters, bonders, linkers,
chipping hammer tinkers.
We of the steel-toe boots
and tough leather gloves.

We are sculptors of giant bones,
builders of skeletons
whose silhouettes rise upward
through bright bursting sparks
to border a boundless orange sky.

We build the bones that hold the shell.
We are the wizards of the weld.

CARPENTERS
B. J. Lee

When our foreman has a task,
all he has to do is ask.

We nail it!

Wooden forms to hold concrete,
built-in benches—take a seat!
Stairways, scaffolds, molding, doors,
framing, bracing, walkways, floors—

We nail it!

Our jobs are as important
as those who raise steel beams.
You take away us carpenters,
you dash skyscraper dreams.

We nail it!

PLUMBERS
Charles Ghigna

We lay pipes
Straight and round.
Inside. Outside.
Up and down.

From the basement
To the top.
We plumb, plumb, plumb.
We never stop.

Cutting. Fitting.
Each new pipe.
Measure twice
To get it right.

Beneath the floors.
Rows by rows.
Behind sealed walls
Water flows.

We take turns.
Work long hours.
Plumbing sinks.
Installing showers.

Safety sprinklers.
Toilets, too.
Lobby fountains
To welcome you.

We take our time.
We do not race.
We set each pipe
In perfect place.

Floor by floor
We spend our days.
We build, build, build
An iron maze.

CONSTRUCTION PROJECT MANAGER

Matt Forrest Esenwine

I'm watching workers hoist and climb.
What worries me the most today:
we've got to get this built on time!

Deadlines set. No overtime!
We need to move that mud and clay!
I'm watching workers hoist and climb.

Every dollar, every dime—
I count the bills we need to pay.
We've got to get this built on time!

Bolts and girders, dust and grime;
pipes were fitted yesterday.
I'm watching workers hoist and climb.

Hammers sing, ratchets chime—
everything looks A-OK!
We've got to get this built on time!

I tap my fingers, hum a rhyme . . .
what makes me happiest today?
I'm watching workers hoist and climb—
we're going to get this built on time!

GLAZIERS
Joan Bransfield Graham

With patient skill,
  we measure,
cut, and size—
  to give this
growing building
  high-rise eyes.
A sweeping
  panorama . . .
look, if you dare.
  Our gift—
a front row seat
  up in the air.

We've put each perfect
  pane of glass
in place . . .
  to help you see
sky's ever-changing
  face.

ELEVATOR INSTALLERS

Lee Bennett Hopkins

We squeeze into
tight cramped corners
inside confined crawl spaces
assembling
suspension cables,
hydraulic buffers,
a well-constructed
landing door.

We install cages
to elevate
or descend you
with a push of a button
without delay
from one floor
to another
day after day
after day.

ELECTRICIANS
J. Patrick Lewis

Master and apprentice technicians,
the nation's hot-wire magicians,
work to empower the dark
tower with a signature mark—
its star on the city skyline
with a beautiful billion-watt shine.
They'll tell you that, barring a glitch,
there's nothing like flipping the switch.

WHAT I AM
Rebecca Kai Dotlich

A storied tower
called
    splendid

etched with echoes
of chatter and shouts,
an iron chime of voices,
topped by a slender slant
piercing the bluest of skies.

Majestic with steel spine;

once known

      as *blueprint*

now part of a
      breathtaking
      spectacular

      skyline.